EARLY INTERMEDIATE LEVEL

# Color Wheel

SIX ORIGINAL PIANO SOLOS

BY MONA REJINO

ISBN 978-1-4950-8055-5

Visit Hal Leonard Online at
**www.halleonard.com**

Contact us:
**Hal Leonard**
7777 West Bluemound Road
Milwaukee, WI 53213
Email: info@halleonard.com

In Europe, contact:
**Hal Leonard Europe Limited**
42 Wigmore Street
Marylebone, London, W1U 2RN
Email: info@halleonardeurope.com

In Australia, contact:
**Hal Leonard Australia Pty. Ltd.**
4 Lentara Court
Cheltenham, Victoria, 3192 Australia
Email: info@halleonard.com.au

# From the Composer

Throughout history composers have seen colors in music, and they strive to bring those colors alive in their compositions. Our world is filled with color. From all aspects of nature to an array of manmade colors, we see and feel the difference color makes in our lives every day on the earth.

***Color Wheel*** explores both the primary and secondary colors, with a piece of music written to express how each of those colors moves me. I hope that you will enjoy exploring the richness and texture of each color through the marvelous medium of music.

*–Mona Rejino*

## *PRIMARY COLORS*

*Sunny Yellow* conveys a feeling of cheerfulness and joy throughout. From the first note to the last, it shares a sense of happiness and well-being.

Blue has been called a mysterious color, and it is the rarest color found in nature. *Elusive Blue* expresses that sense of wonder with a tender melody and poignant harmonies.

Red is considered the boldest of all colors, conveying a feeling of excitement. In *Vibrant Red*, the pianist finds a dazzling showpiece to perform with confidence and exuberant energy.

## *SECONDARY COLORS*

The color green is made of blue and yellow, creating a soothing tone. *Cool Green* has a casual, relaxed feel to it, but a little humor spills over from the yellow tint.

The color orange is anything but shy, a brilliant mixture of yellow and red. Through the use of mixed meter and a dancelike melody, *Sassy Orange* makes a statement all its own.

Purple is my favorite color, a lovely combination of blue and red creating a rich, royal hue. *Majestic Purple* takes you on a regal journey filled with dreams and fantasies.

CONTENTS

# Cool Green

By Mona Rejino

Laid back (♩ = 112)

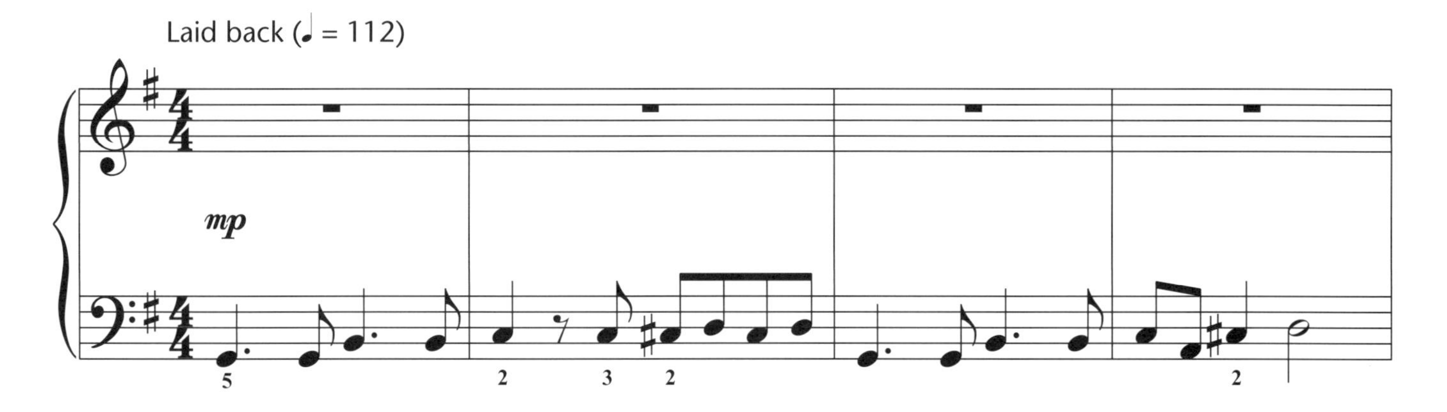

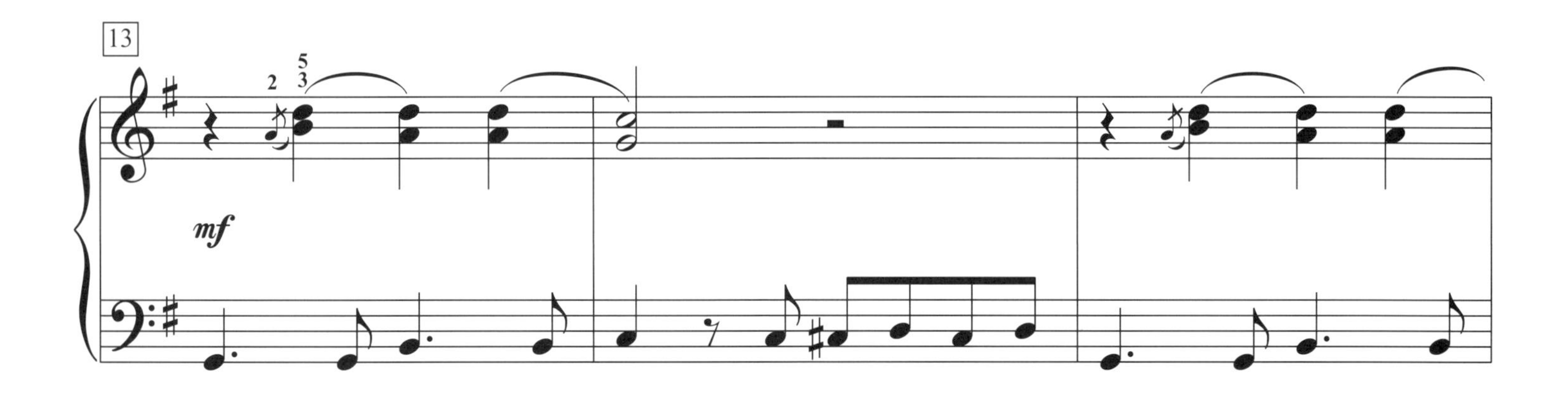

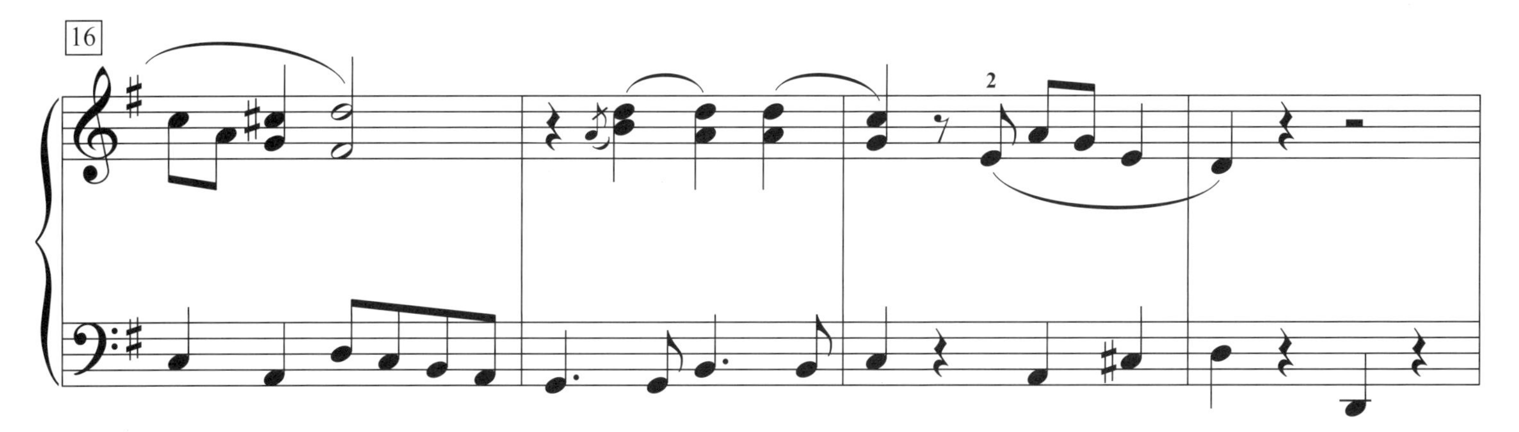
16

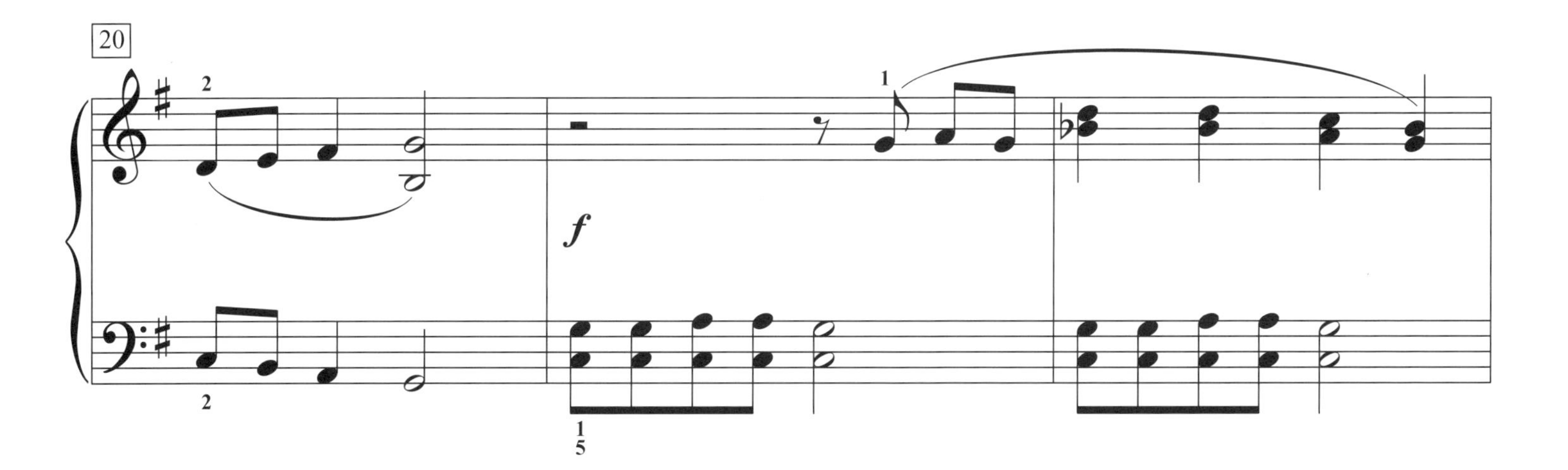
20
f

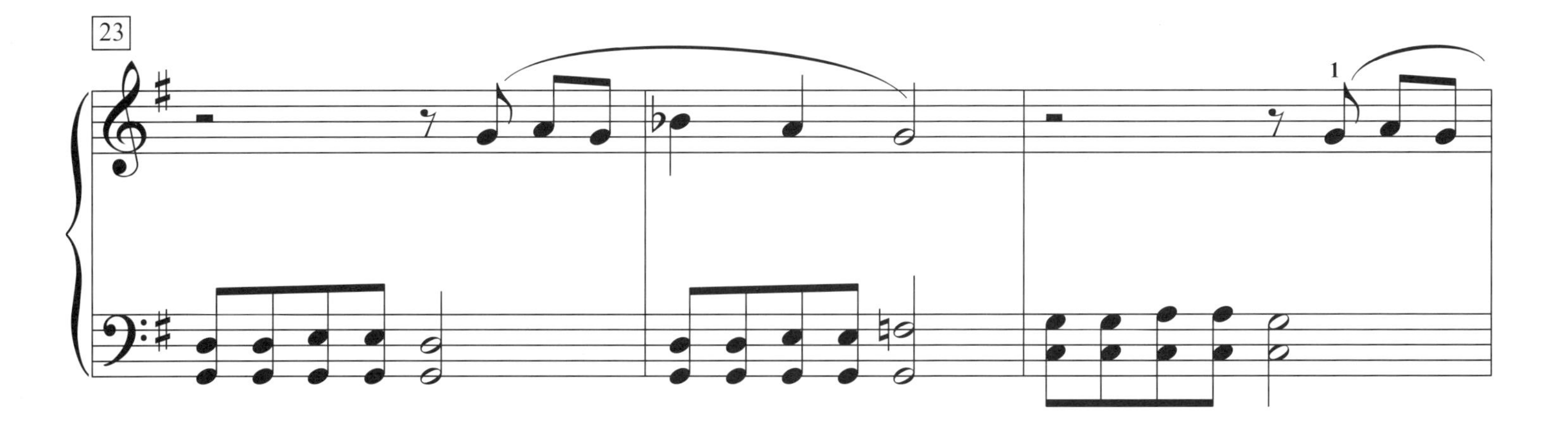
23

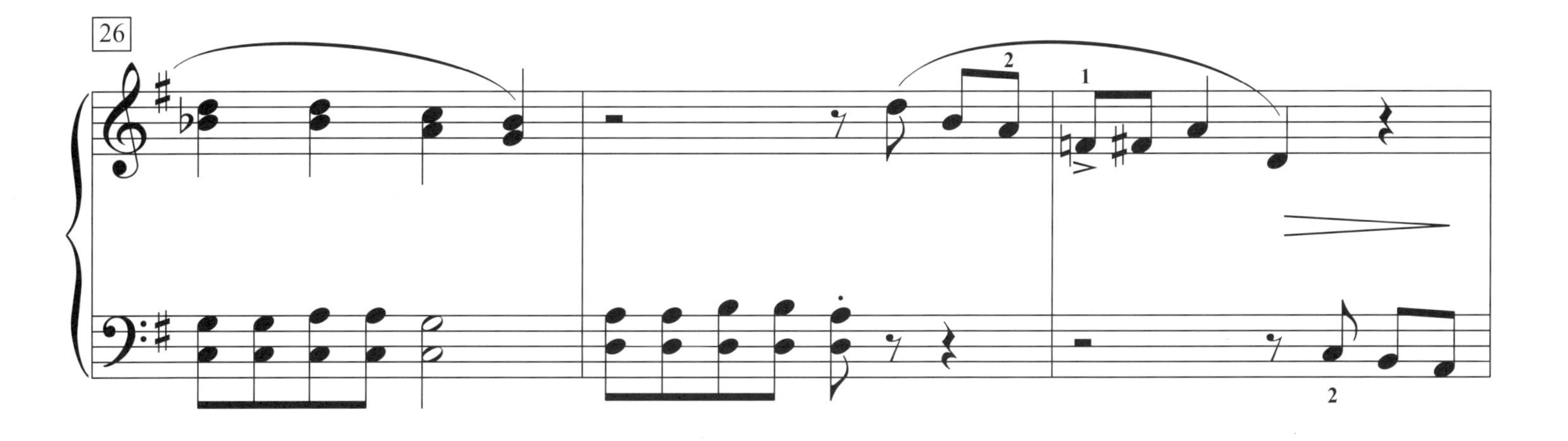
26

29
5
3
mp

32
2

35
4
2
4
1
cresc.
mf
5
3
2
1
2
1

38
rit.
p
5
3
2
1
2
1

# Elusive Blue

By Mona Rejino

Tenderly, with expression (♩ = 112)

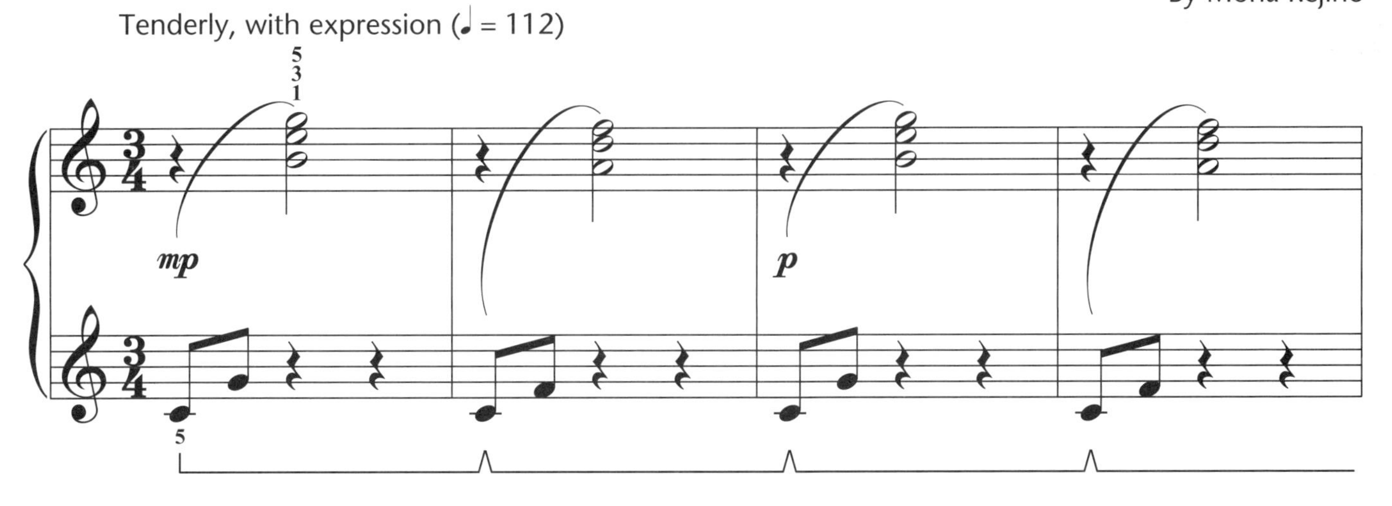

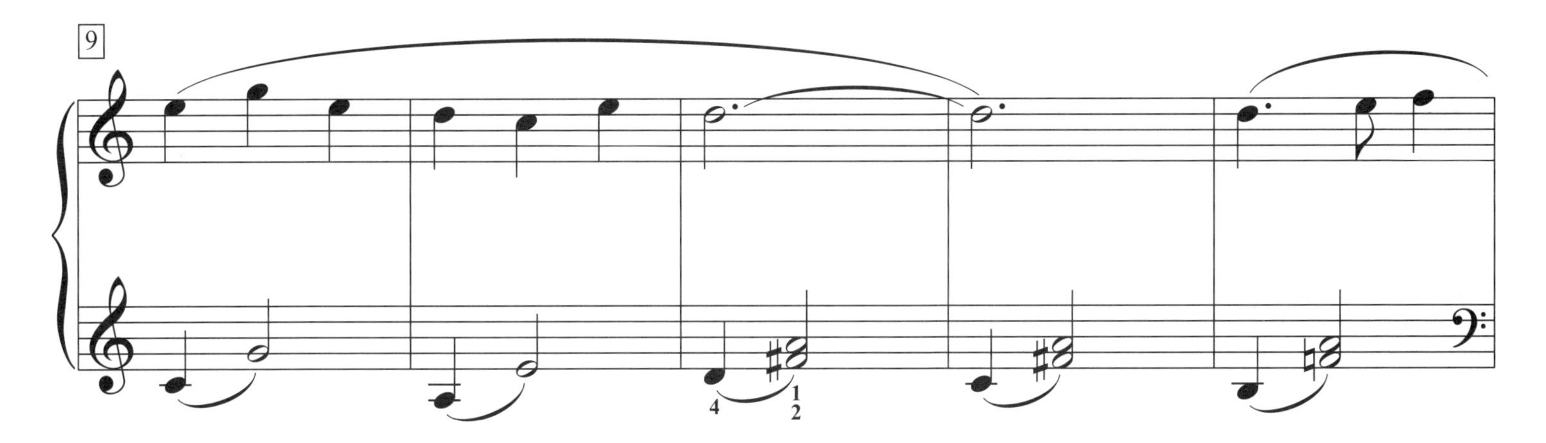


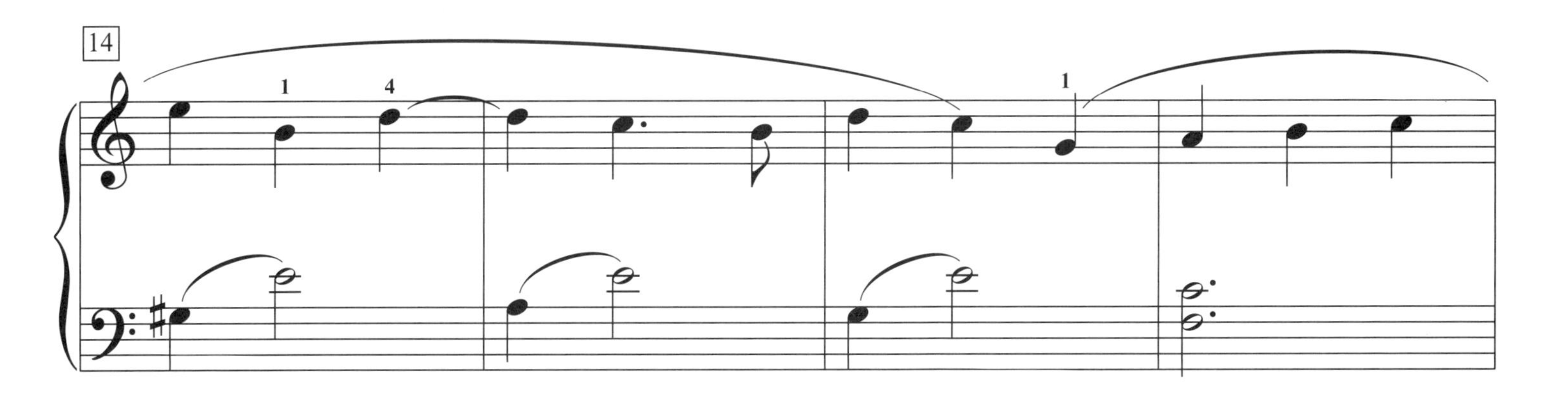

18
mf

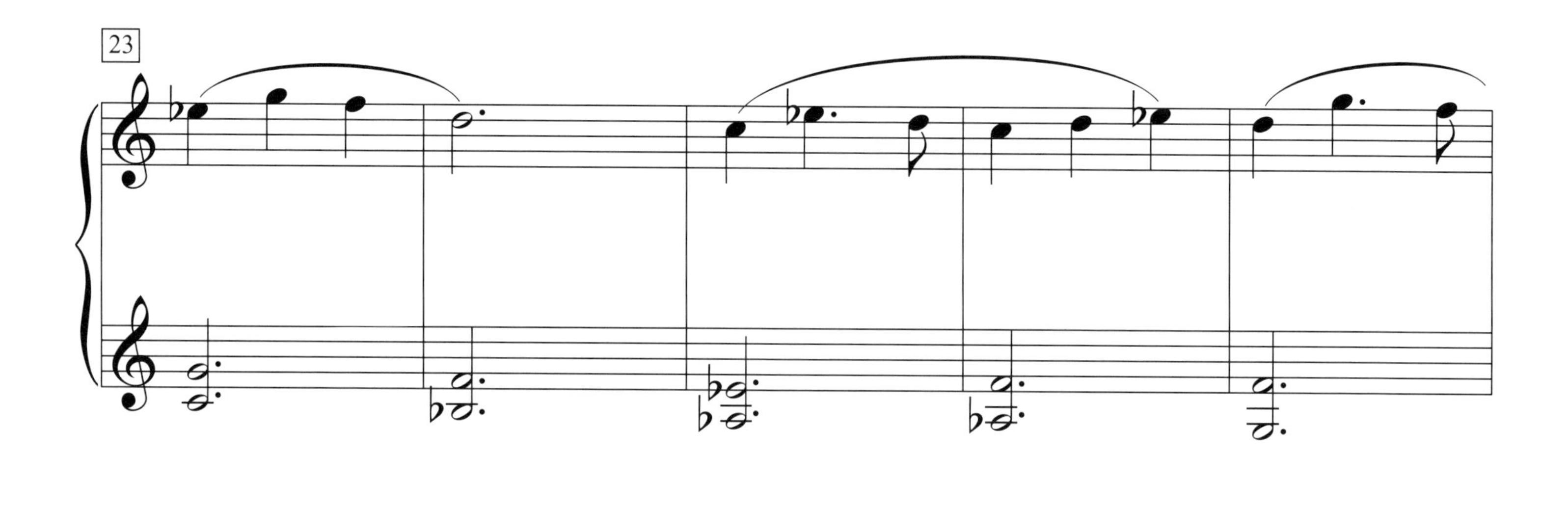
23

28
poco rit.
mp a tempo

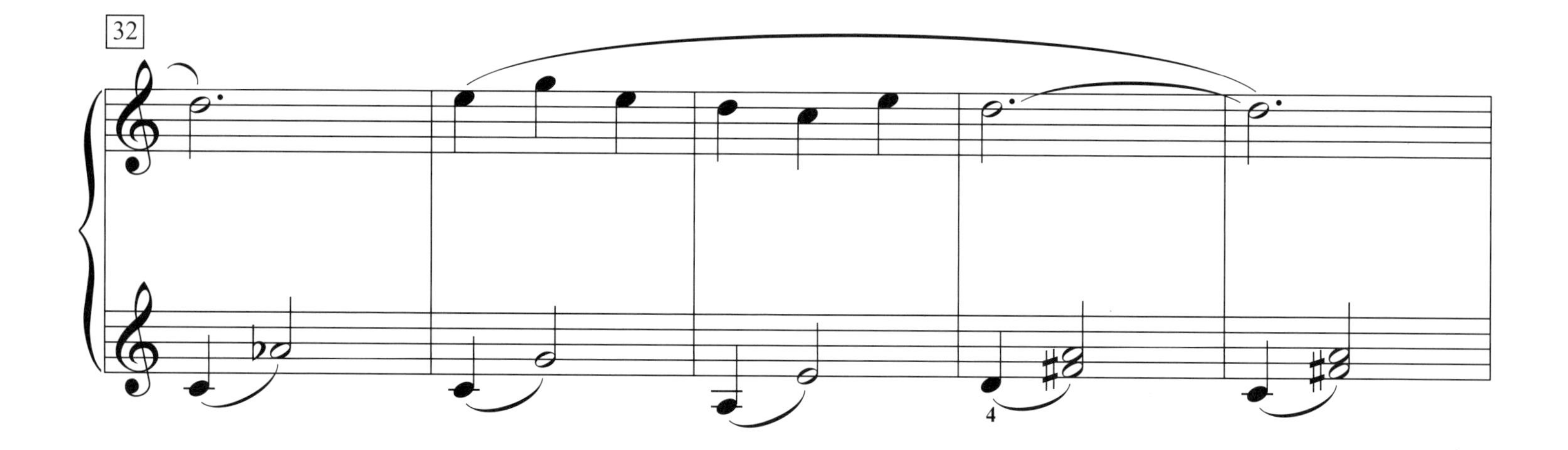
32

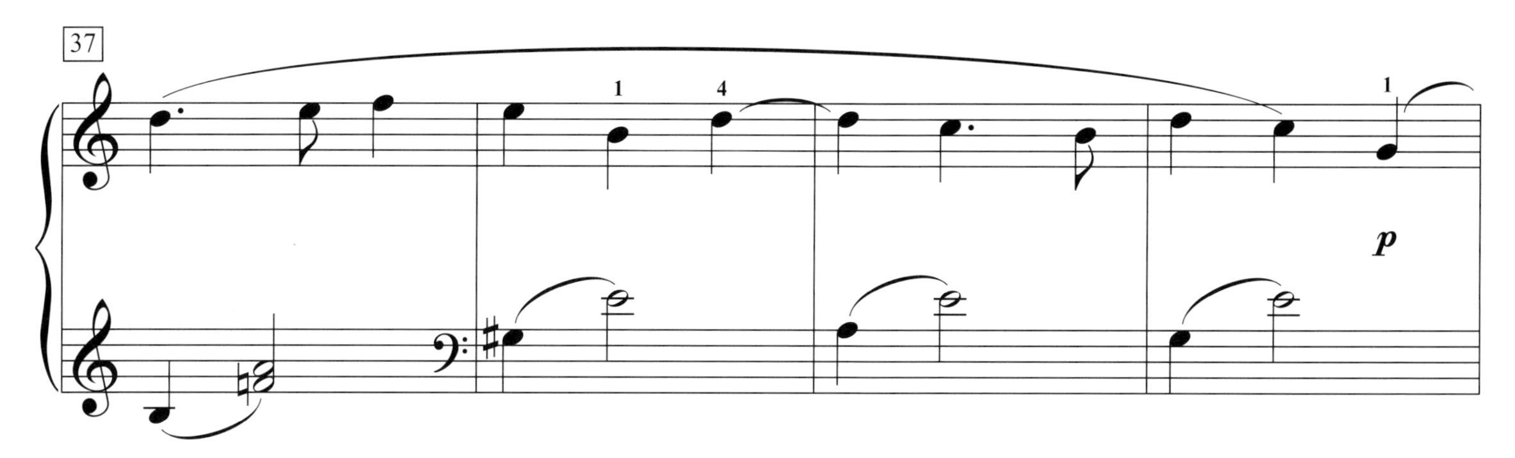
37
1
4
1
p

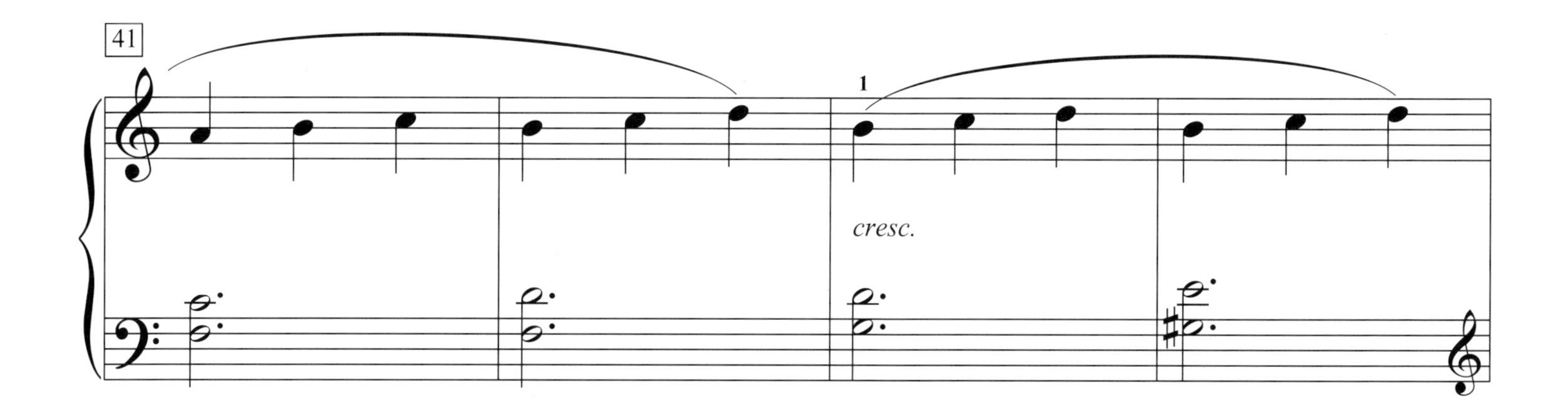
41
1
cresc.

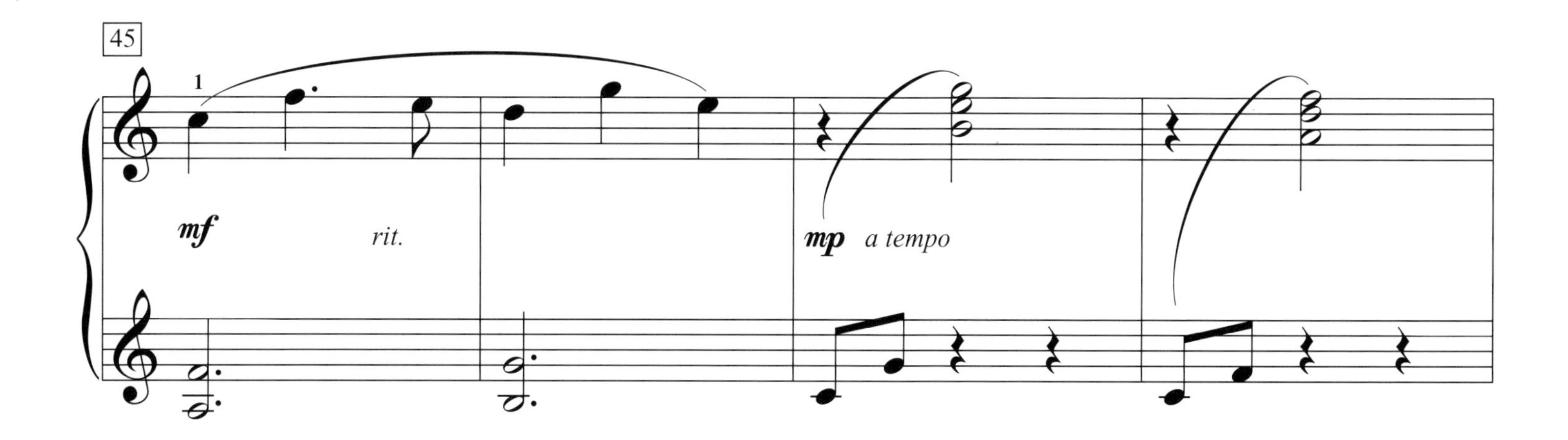
45
1
mf
rit.
mp
a tempo

49
8va
p
rit.
p

# Majestic Purple

By Mona Rejino

Flowing, with freedom (♩ = 126)

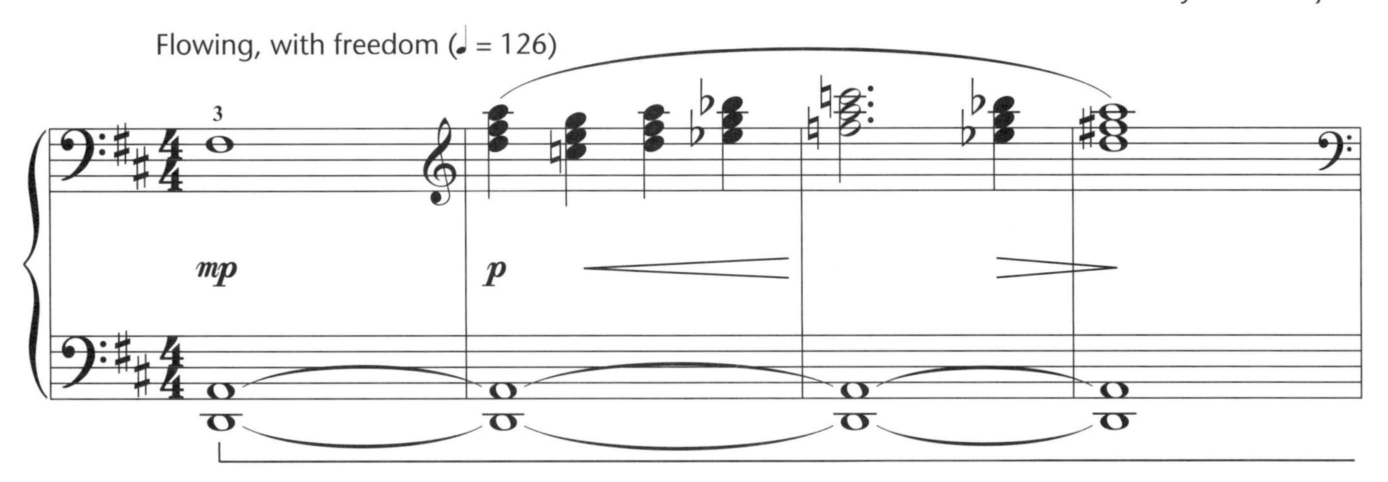


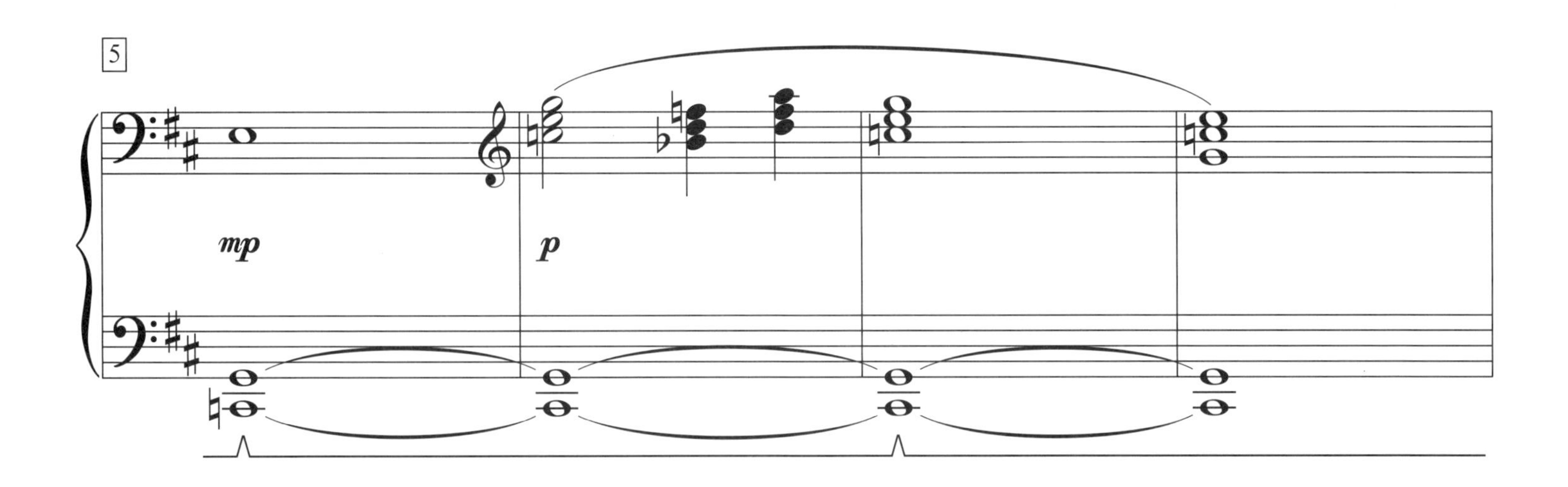


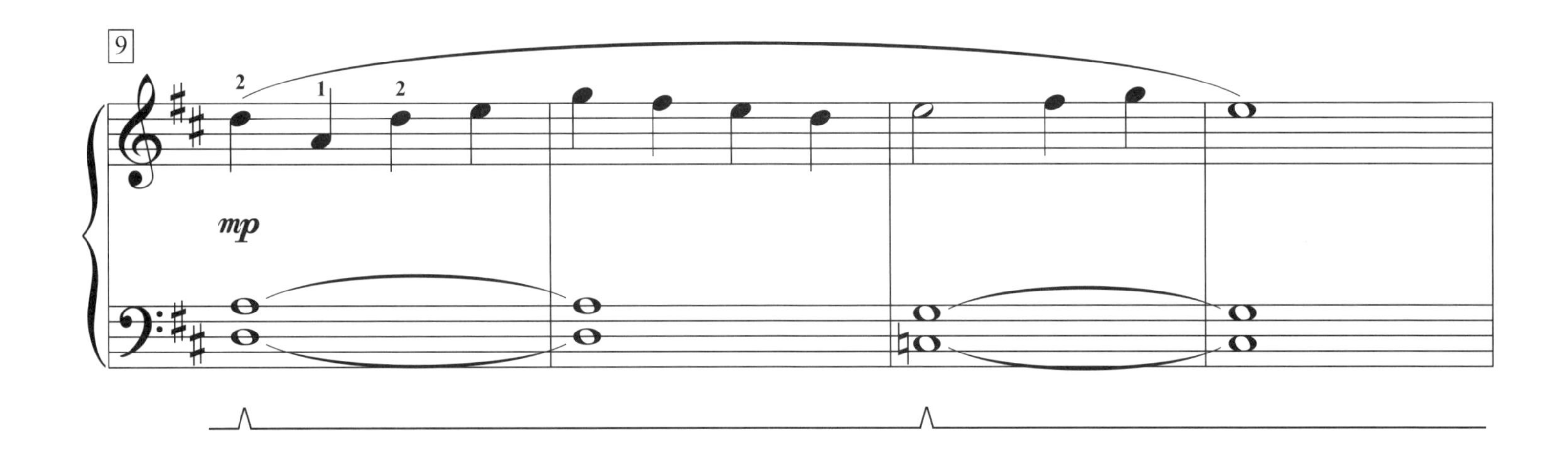

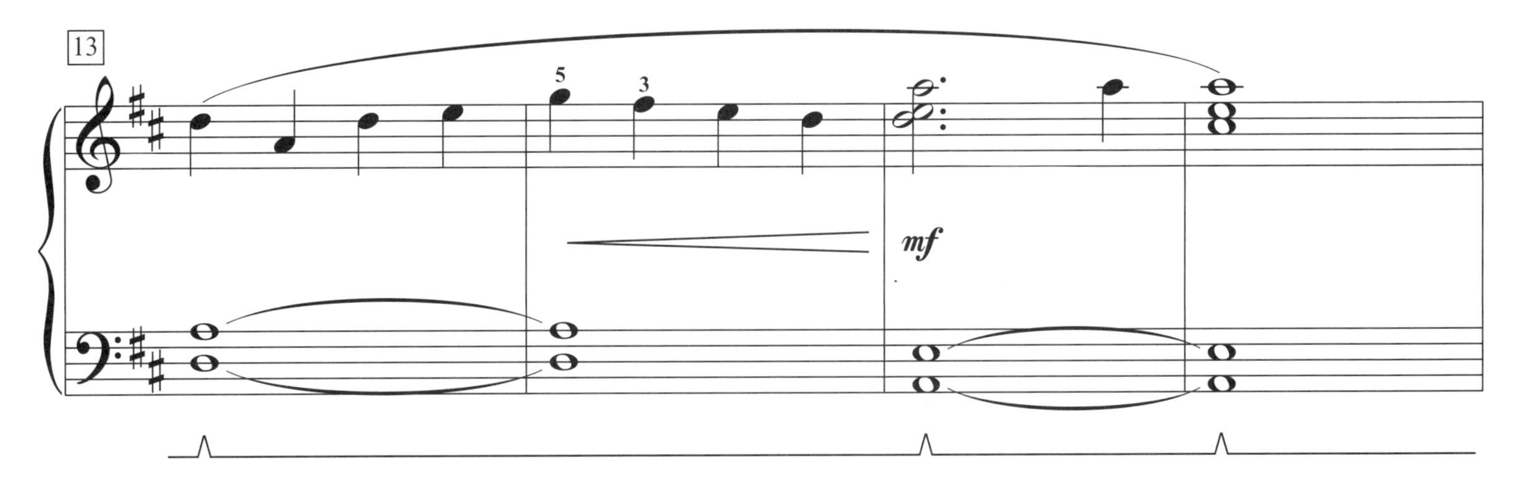
13
mf

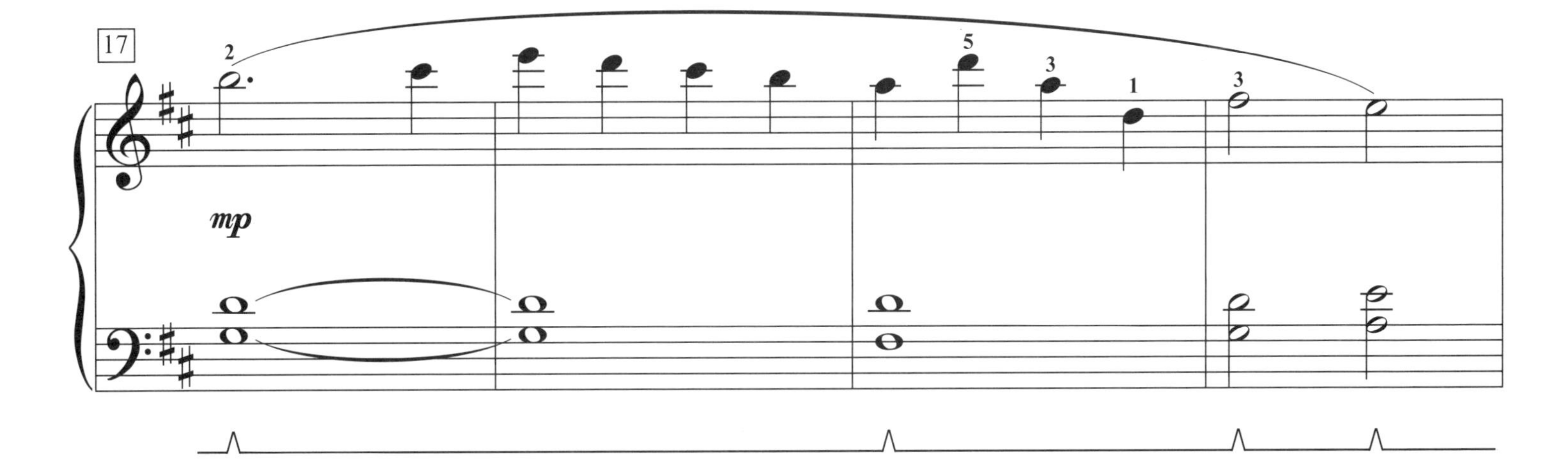
17
mp

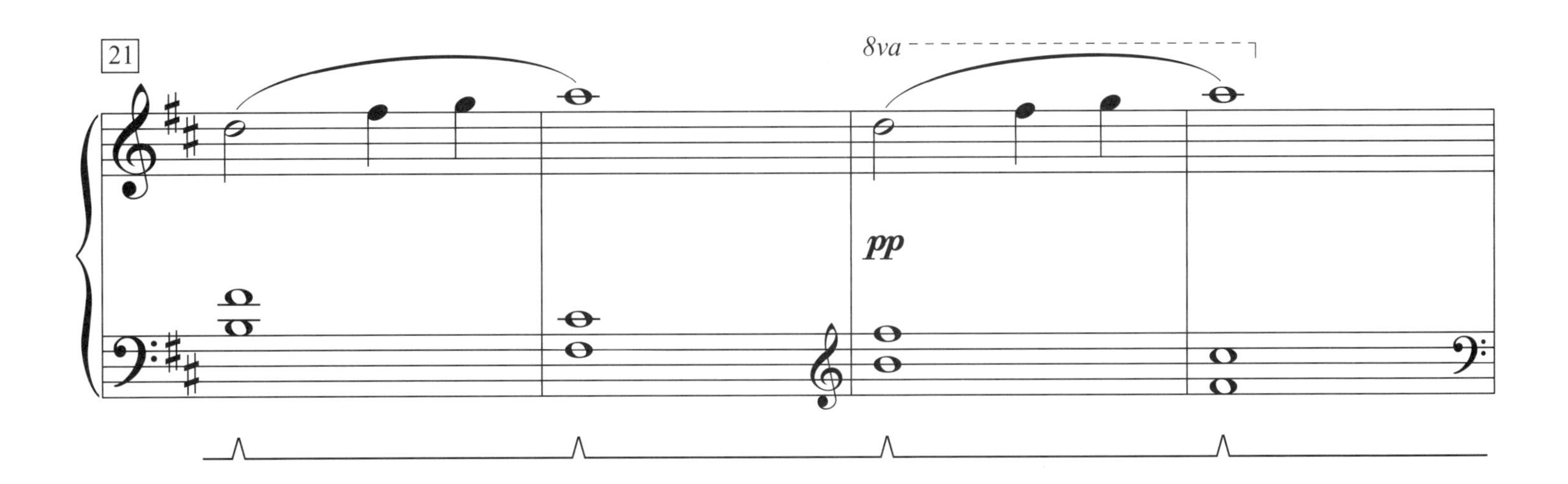
21
8va
pp

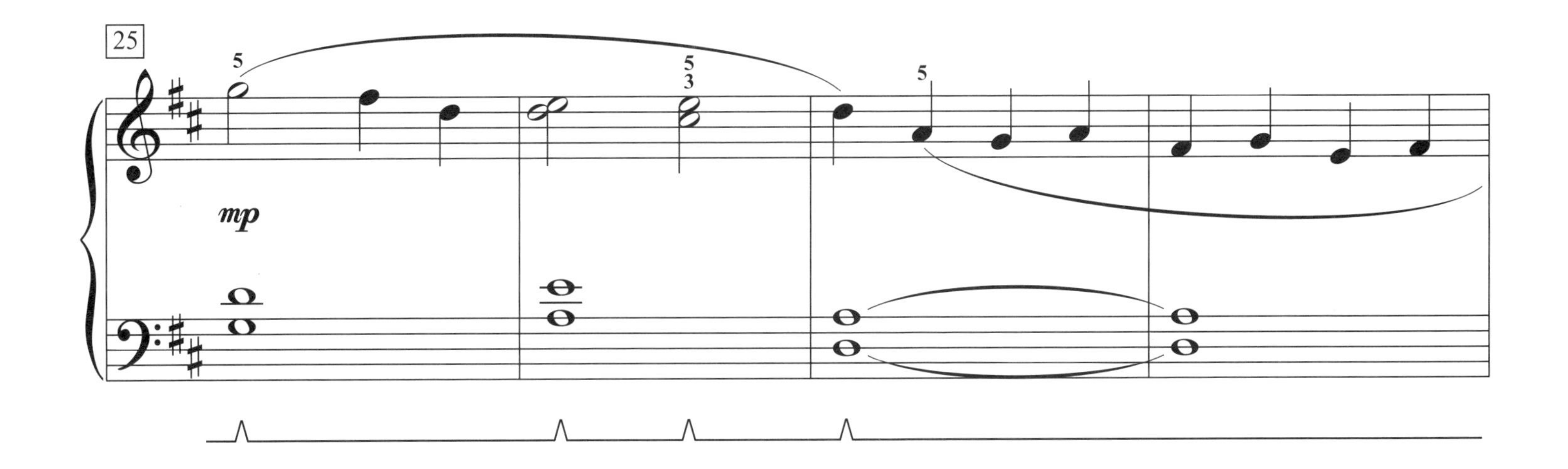
25
mp

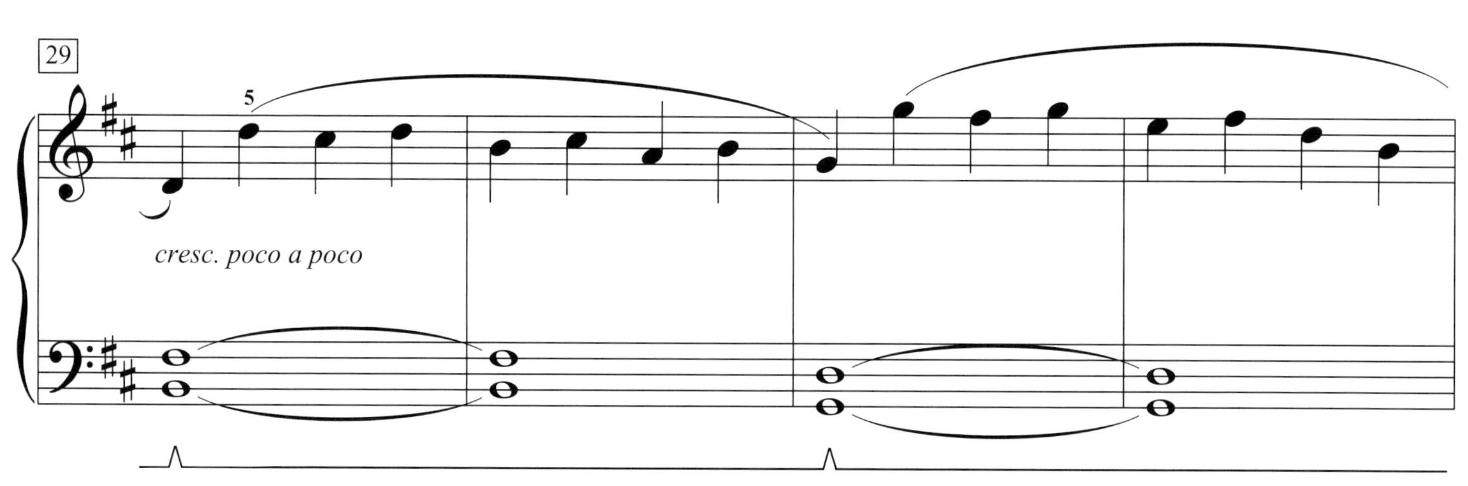
29
5
cresc. poco a poco

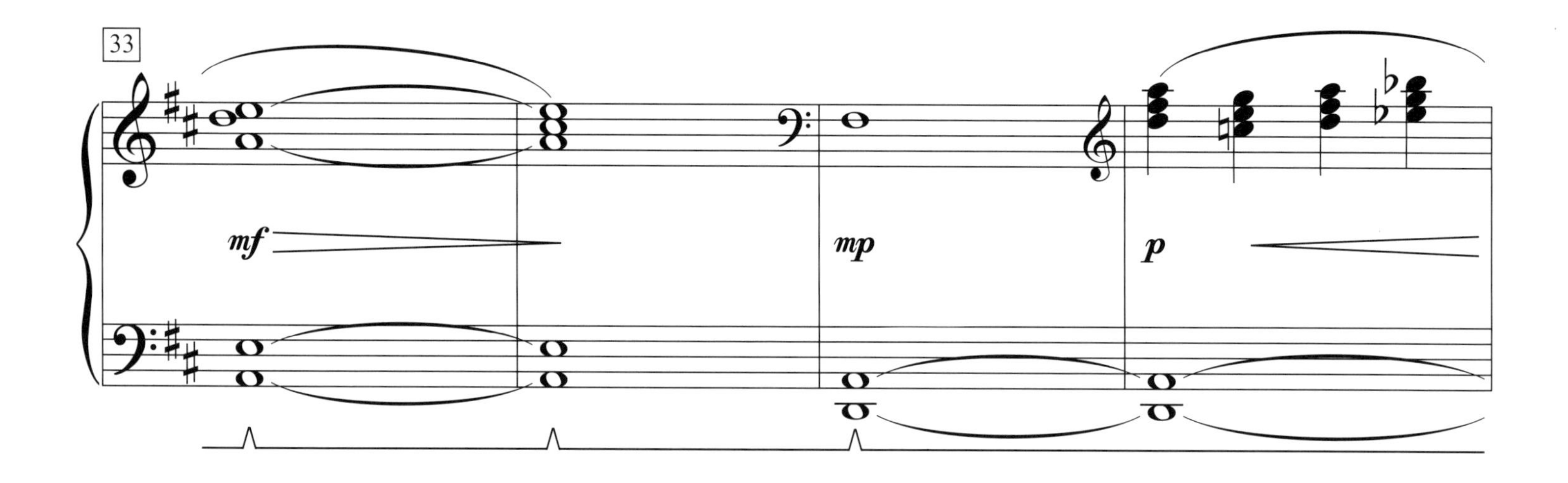
33
mf
mp
p

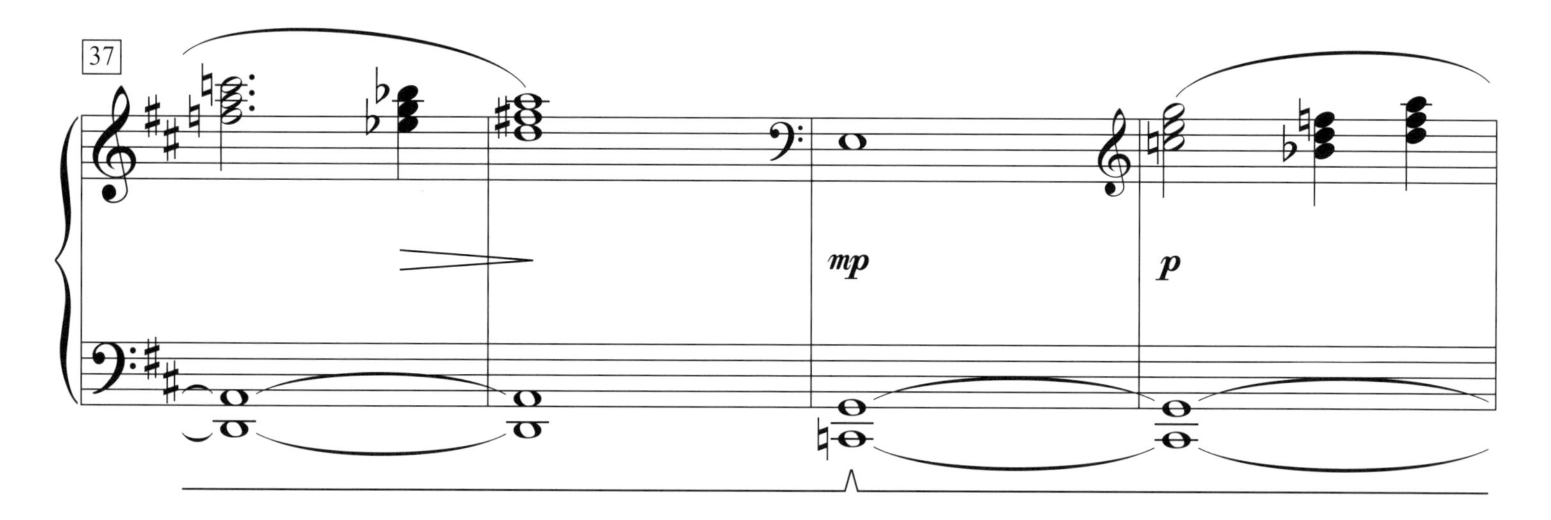
37
mp
p

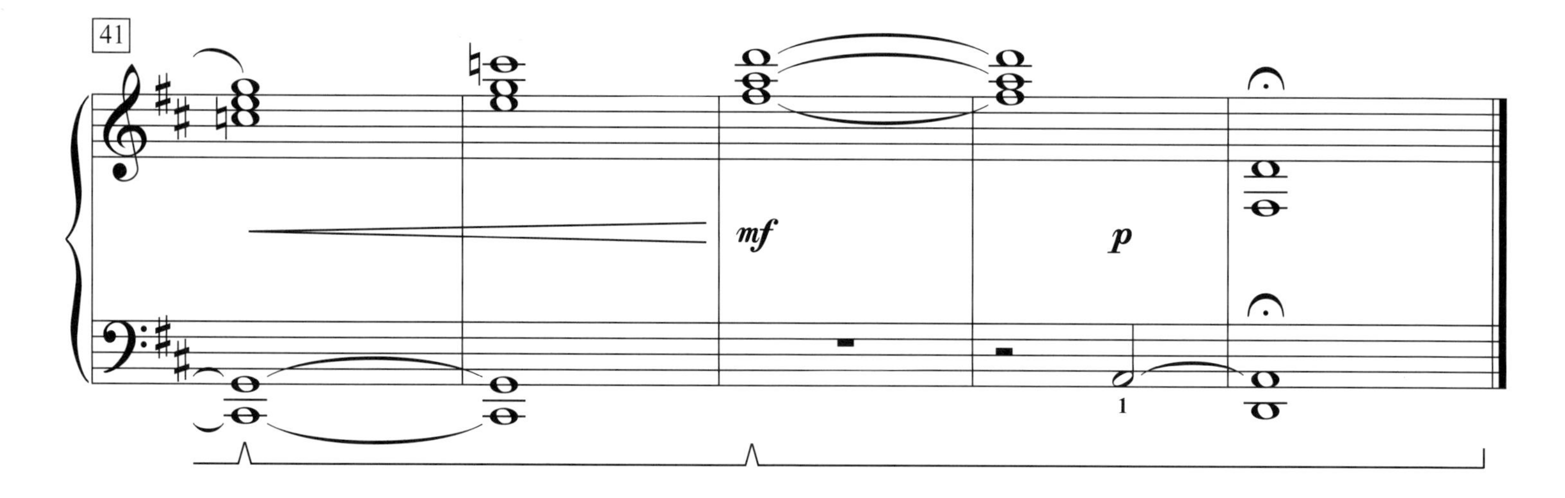
41
mf
p
1

# Sassy Orange

By Mona Rejino

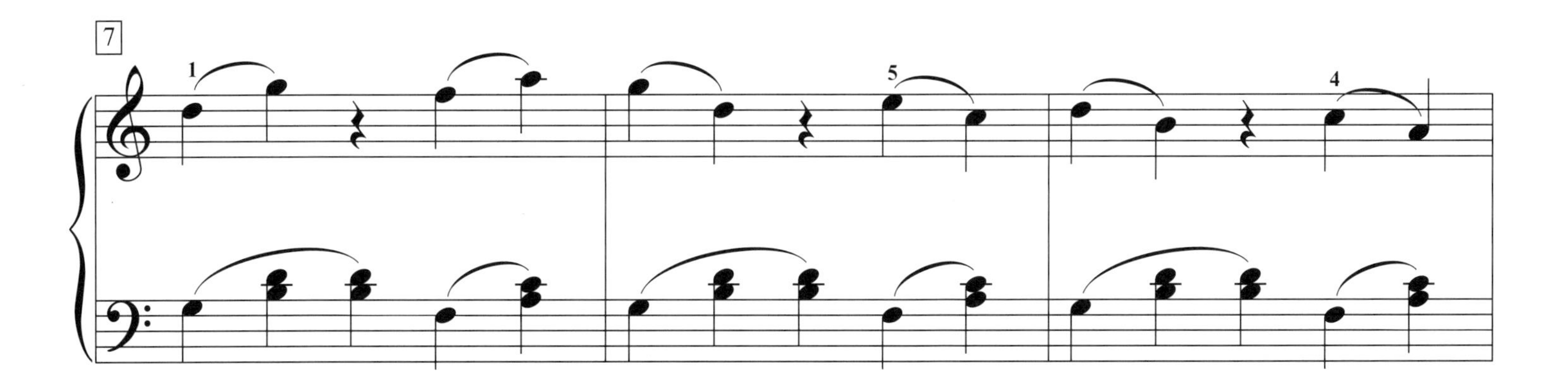


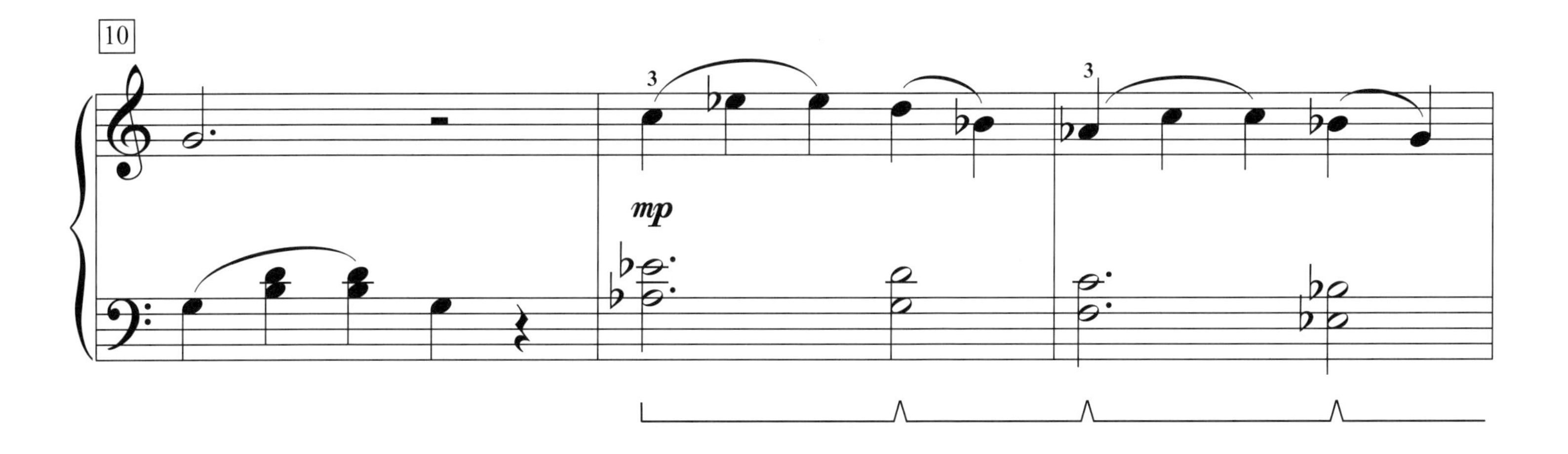

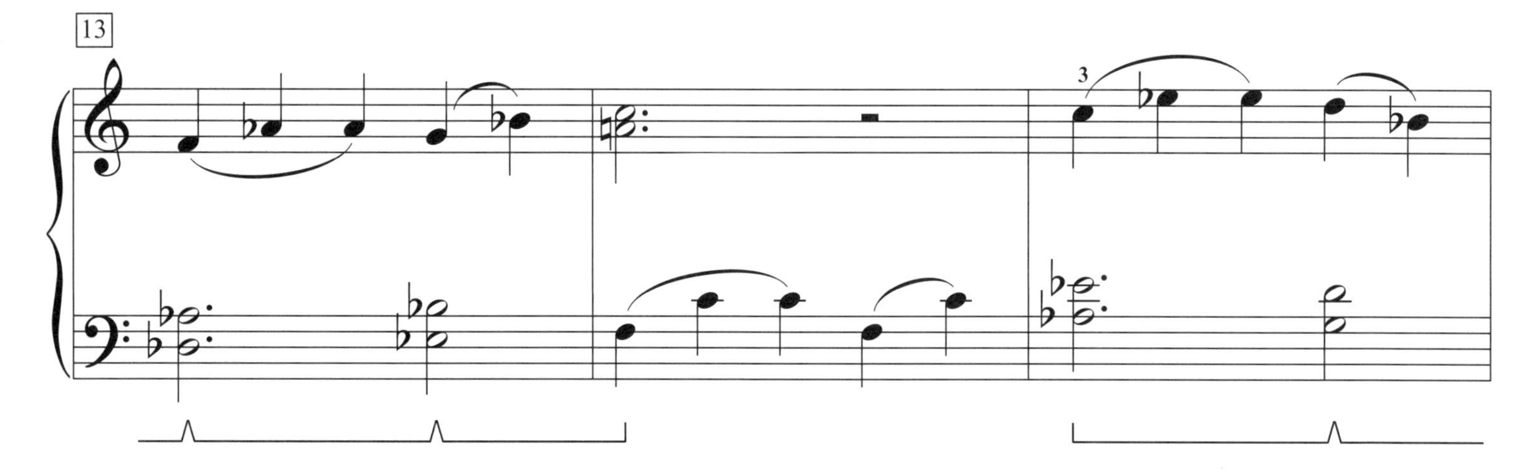
13
3
3

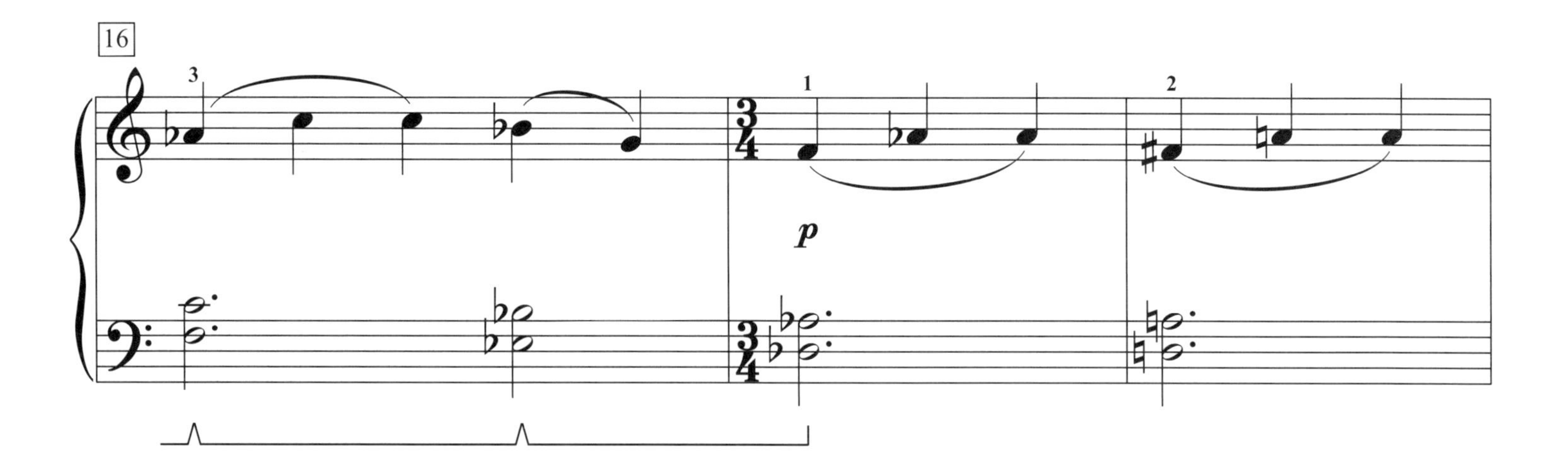
16
3
1
2
p

19
1
2
1
2
cresc. poco a poco

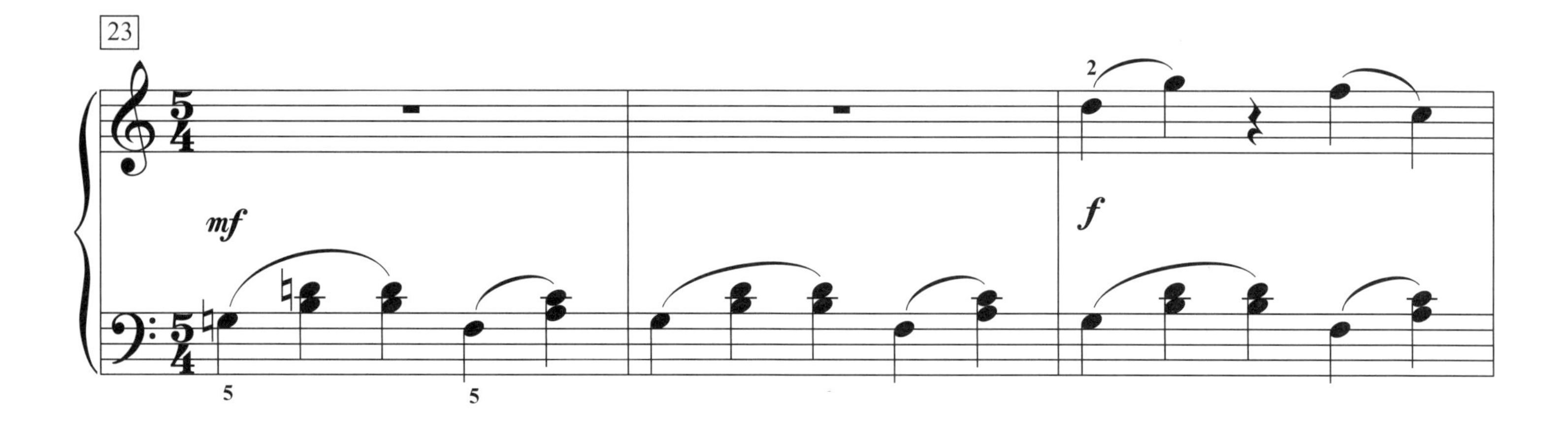
23
2
mf
f
5
5

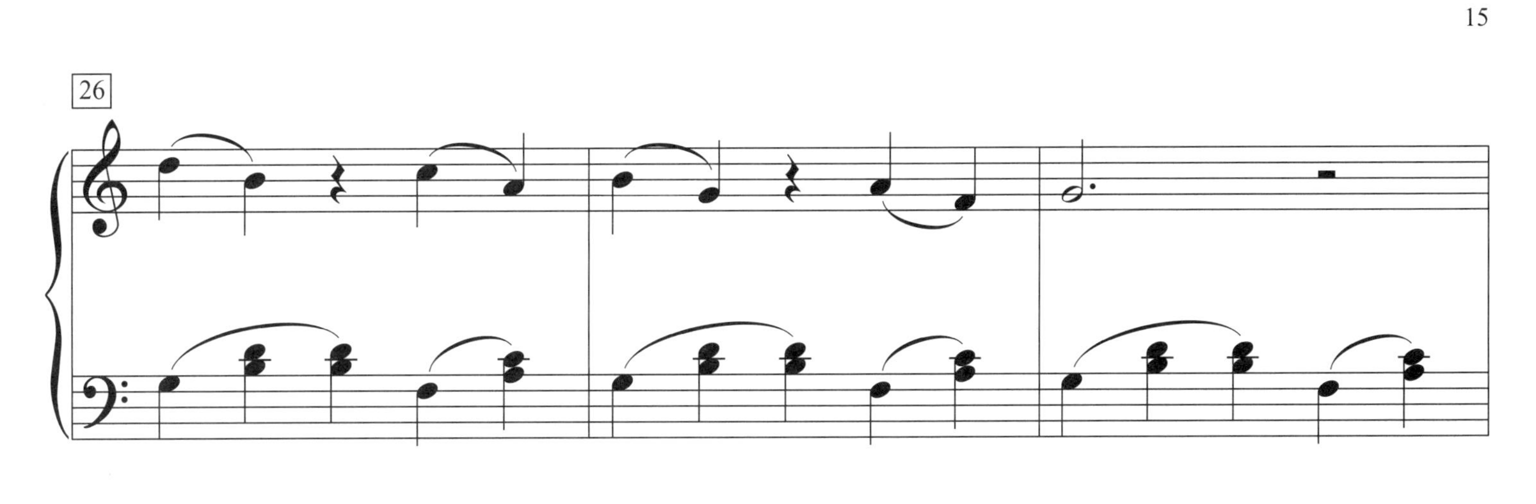
26

29
1

32
mf
mp
p

36
8va
mp
mf
f
ff
8vb

# Sunny Yellow

By Mona Rejino

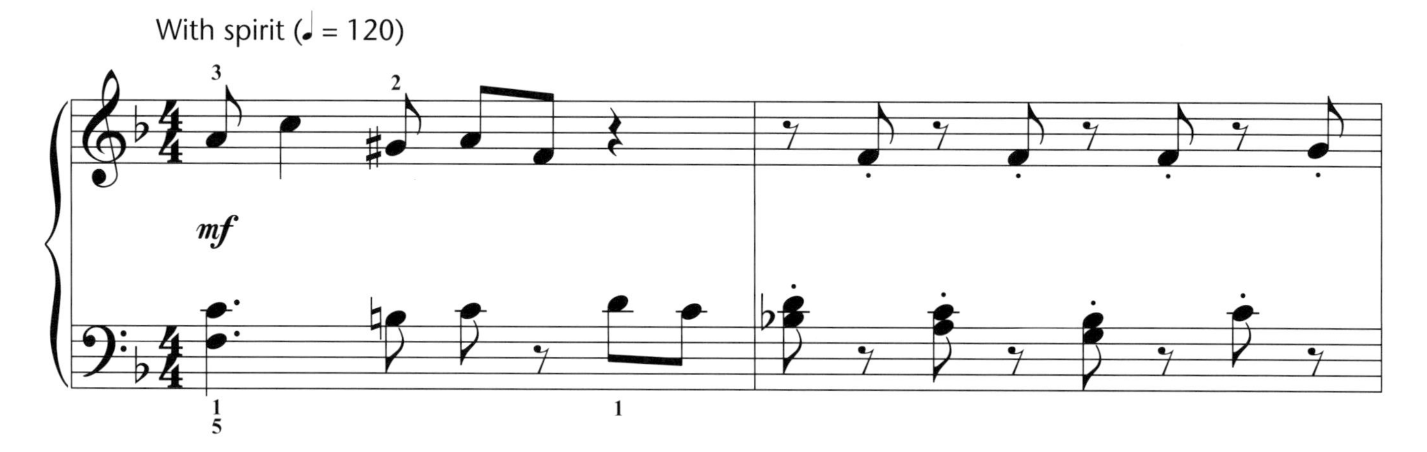


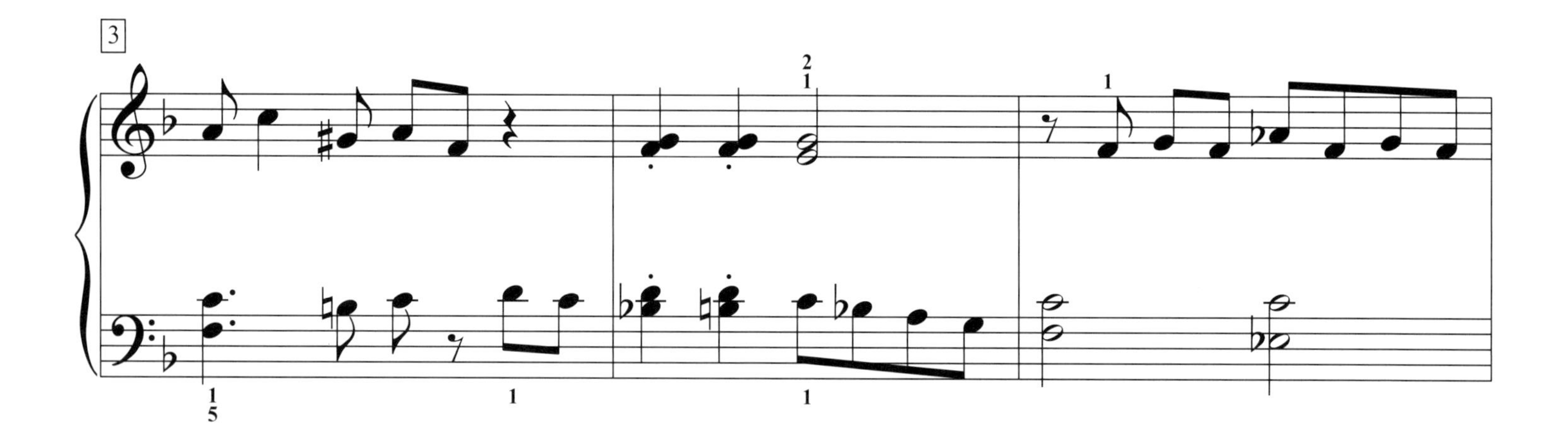

9
L.H.
mp

11
L.H.

13
L.H.

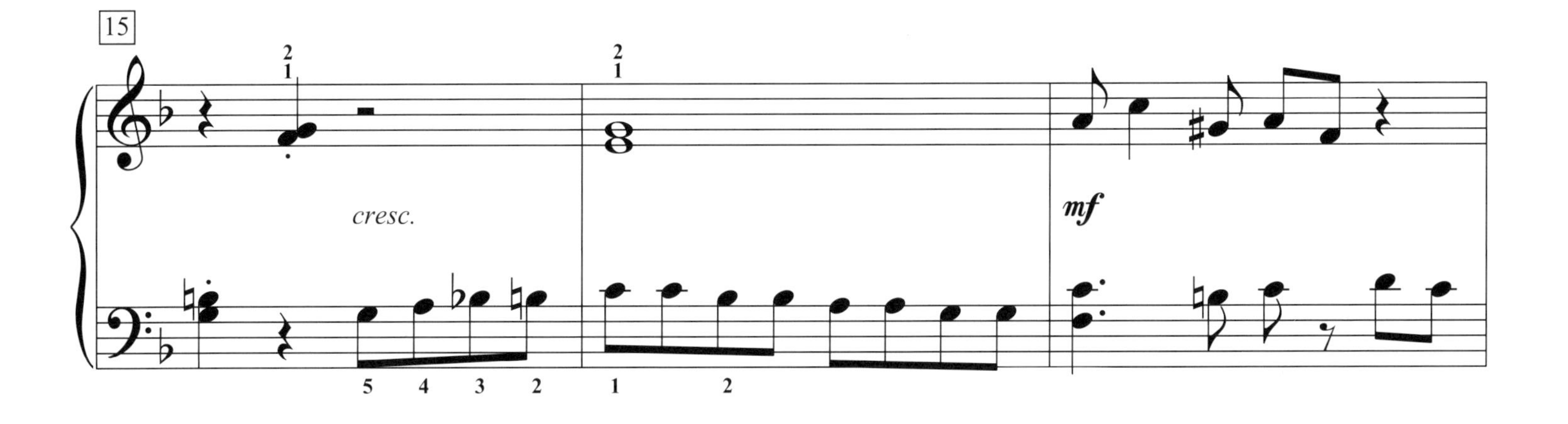
15
cresc.
mf

18

20
p
mp

23
L.H.
mf
mp
rit.

25
L.H.
p
f a tempo

# Vibrant Red

By Mona Rejino

With energy (♩ = 116)

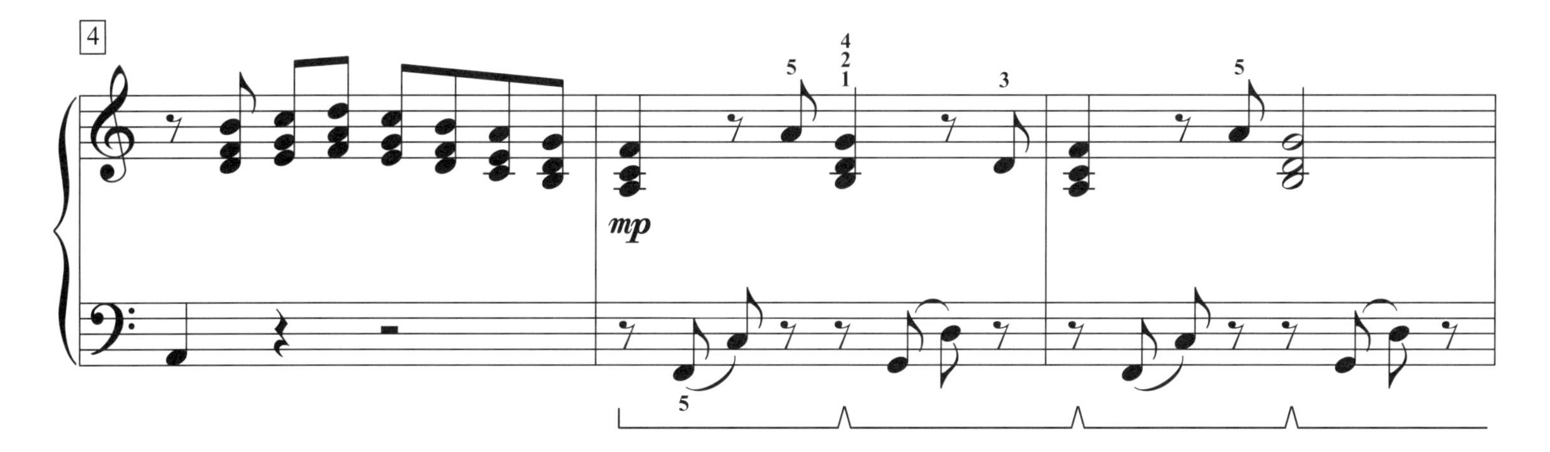

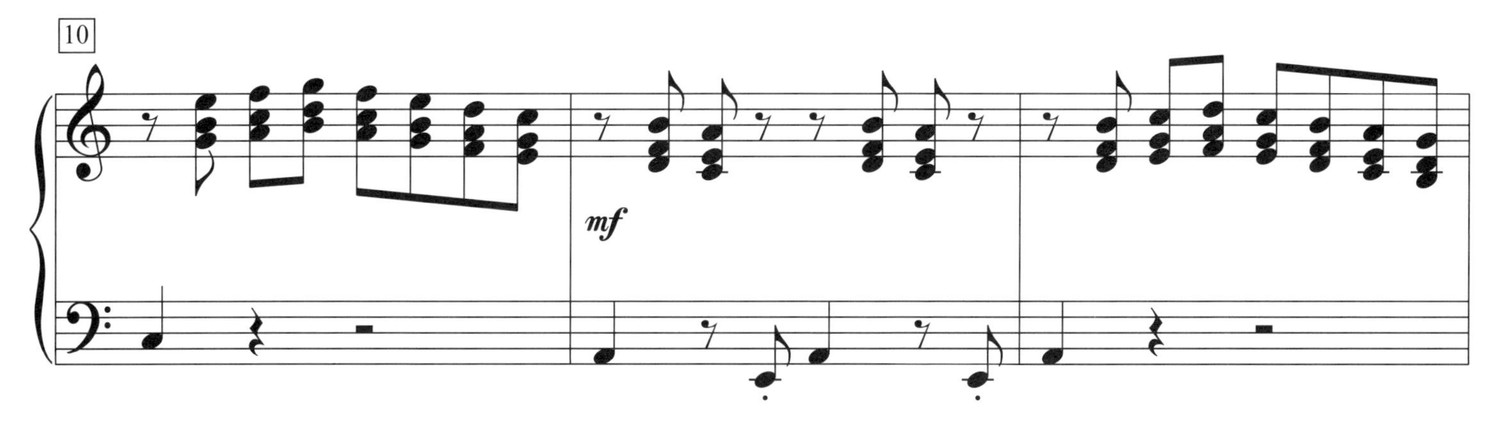

13
mp
cresc.

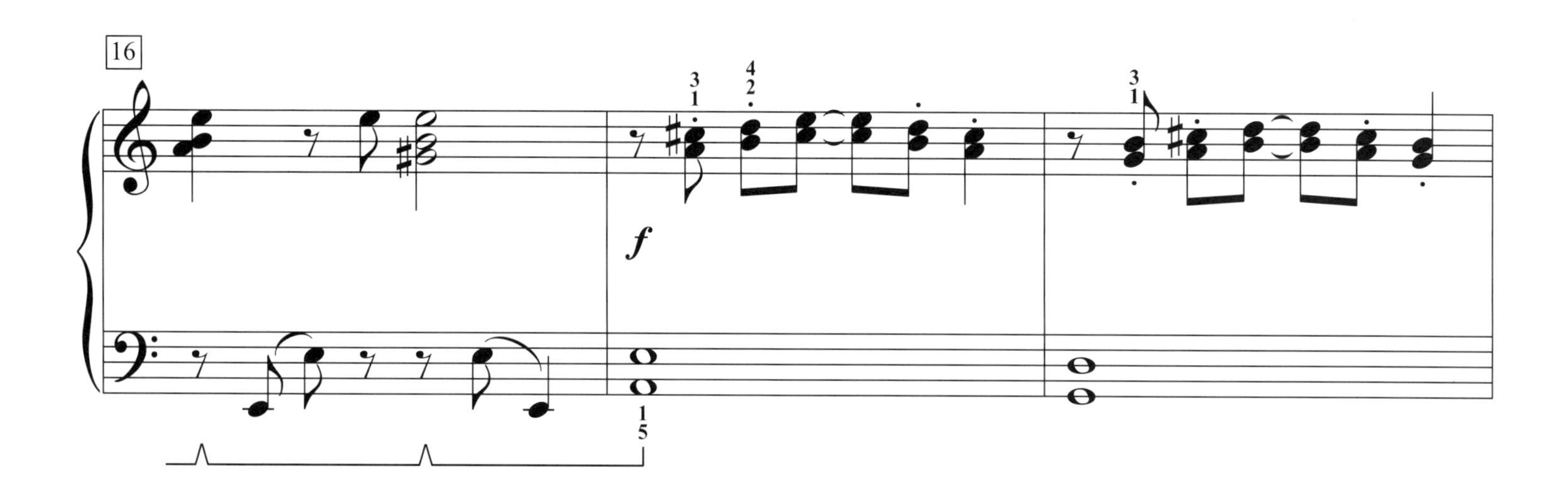
16
f

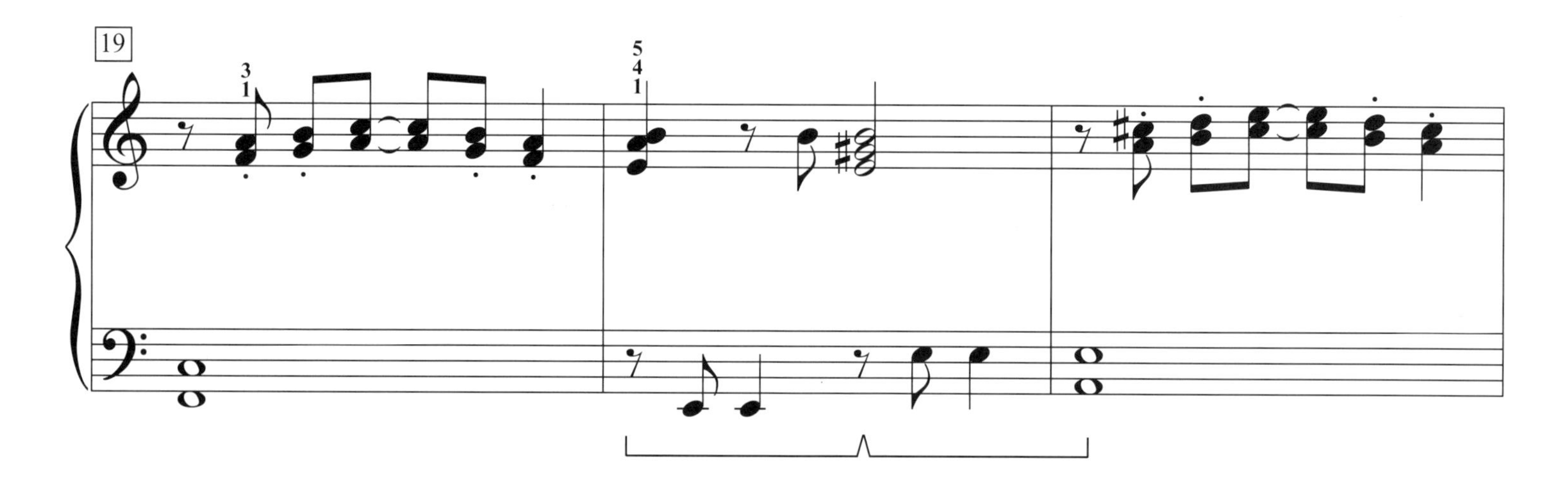
19

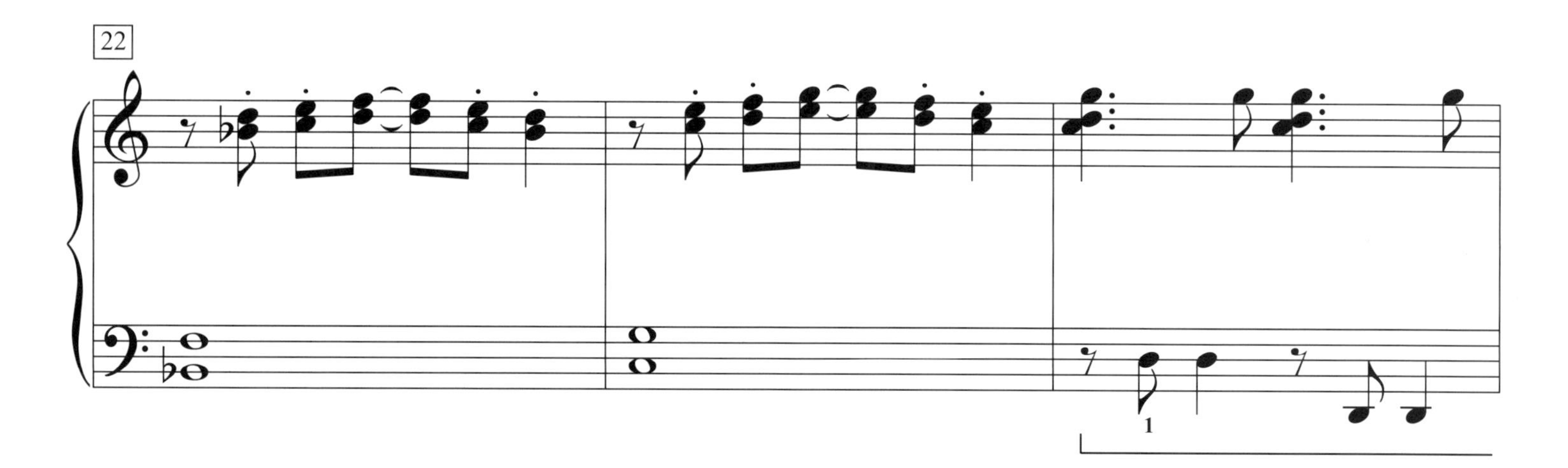
22

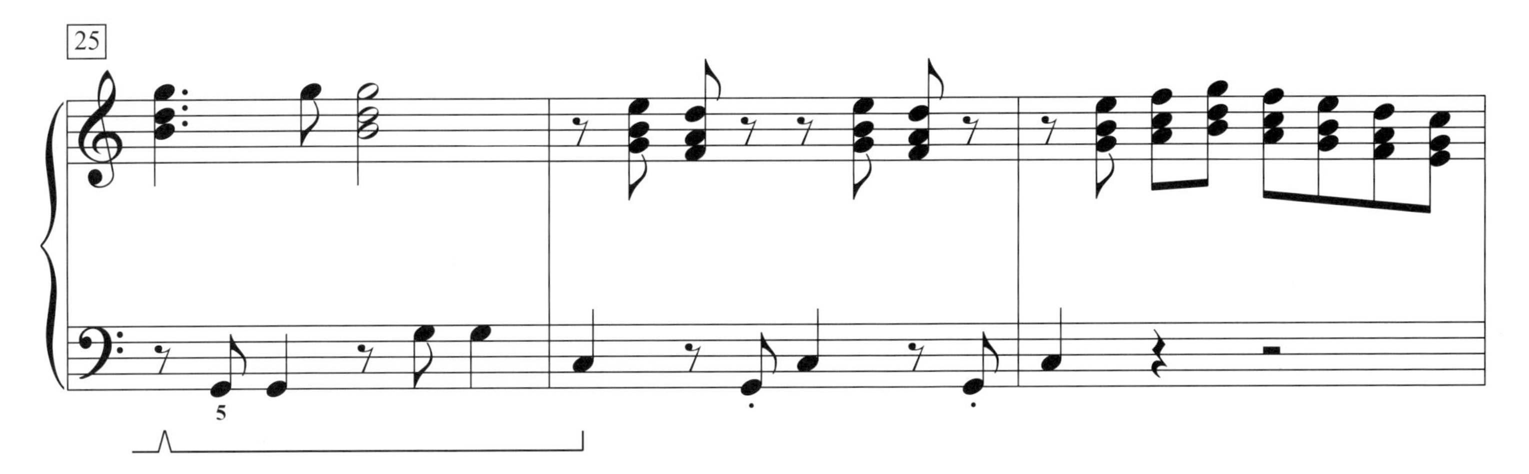
25
5

28
mf
3
mp

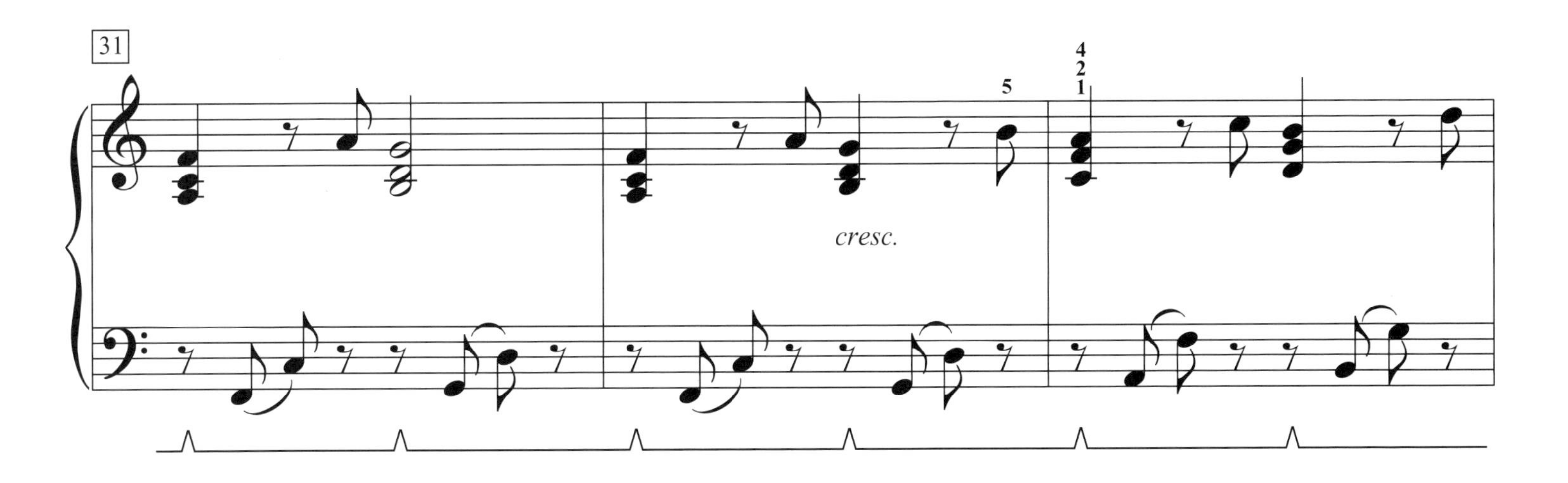
31
5
4
2
1
cresc.

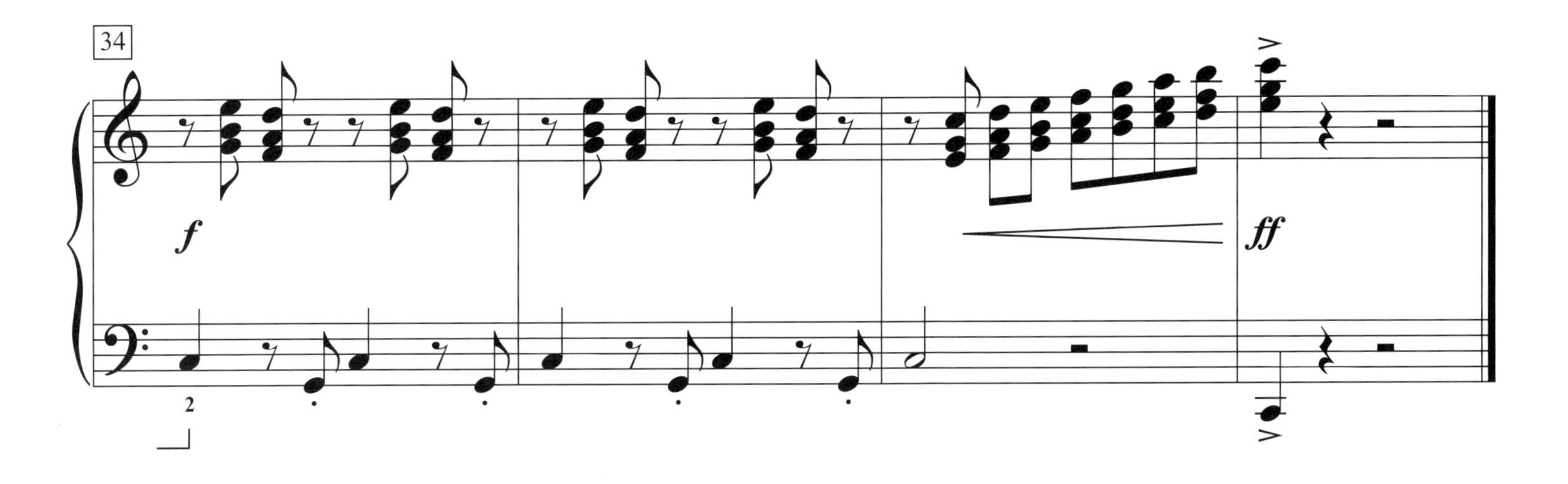
34
f
ff
2

# PIANO THEORY

## BY MONA REJINO

***Essential Elements Piano Theory*** is a comprehensive course designed to help students master theory concepts. New concepts are gradually introduced in a clearly presented format, followed by sufficient and effective reinforcement. Each book features three sections of "Musical Mastery" which include ear training, mastery in rhythm, symbols, reading, and analysis. Students learn to apply their theoretical knowledge in a musical context through such elements as improvisation, transposition, reading lead lines and standard chord progressions. Each book concludes with a section of "Theory Mastery" which includes a review test and ear training. The creative and fun approach of this series applies the student's understanding of theory to real musical examples, and will enhance and supplement any method book.

**LEVEL 1**
00296926.......$6.99

**LEVEL 2**
00296927.......$6.99

**LEVEL 3**
00296928.......$6.99

**LEVEL 4**
00296929.......$6.99

**LEVEL 5**
00123470.......$6.99

**LEVEL 6**
00123472.......$6.99

**www.halleonard.com**

Prices, contents, and availability subject to change without notice.
0317